The Life of Asil

Volume 1

Asil Ttocs

Asil Ttocs

Copyright © 2018 Asil Ttocs
All rights reserved.
ISBN-10: 0615319076
ISBN-13: 978-0615319070

The Life of Asil

DEDICATION

THIS BOOK IS DEDICATED TO SAUNDRA & BILLY SCOTT & ERMA JOE SWEET

THANK YOU TO MY MANY FRIENDS & FAMILY. DARIAN DAVIS, DALLAS, DASH, AUDREY WILSON, VINCENT WILSON, FAITH (COOKIE) SIMMS, MARY WARD, SIOBHAN SCOTT, MICHELLE DUNCAN, TERESA STEWART, KIM FREEMAN, BARBRA & THOMAS HUCKABY, JAYDN FOSTER, SHELIA KNUCKLES, JANET & ART REYNOLDS, ANN DEVUNAY, PHYLLIS COX, GREG GRINER, GREGORY ALEXANDER, PATTY SICULAR, FALLON SINCLAIR, IONIA DUNN LEE, CARLA FISHER, JANET GRAY, GWEN DEVOE, MAHISHA DELLINGER, JANELLE SANDS, STAR JONES, CORYNNE CORBETT, PHYLLIS CUINGTON, MADELINE JONES, PLUS MODEL MAGAZINE, ESSENCE MAGAZINE.

MY ONLINE FRIENDS, @MURDAREPORT (TENESHA) KIM POSTELL, BLOG WITH KIM MASTERMIND GROUP @MINISTEROFSTYLE (CATHY WITTER) @FLUFFYKFIERCE (KAREN) MUCHLOVEFROMNINA @NAKESHADANYEL1 (NAKESHA) @RESARICHARDSON, @ROYALTY_N_MOOR @IM_JUST_JACKIE @OFFICIALREINVENTIONRUNWAY @PHASIONISTA (FRESITA SMITH)

Asil Ttocs

The Life of Asil

CONTENTS

	Acknowledgments	i
1	Chapter One	1
2	Chapter Two	Pg 5
3	Chapter Three	Pg 8
4	Chapter Four	Pg 14
5	Chapter Five	Pg 18
6	Chapter Six	Pg 22
7	Chapter Seven	Pg 26
8	Chapter Eight	Pg 32
9	Chapter Nine	Pg 36
10	Chapter Ten	Pg 42

Asil Ttocs

ACKNOWLEDGMENTS

The Life of Asil is based on a true story
created by Asil Ttocs
Characters by Asil Ttocs
Music & Film by DirectorzInc
Screenplay by Asil Ttocs & GES
Directed by Asil Ttocs

CHAPTER ONE

Asil's mother, Corynne, is turning the bacon over in the frying pan. "Asil! Asil! Come eat your breakfast. It's getting late!" Asil is packing her backpack with workout gear for her cheerleader tryouts after school. "Okay, momma, I'm coming! Asil grabs her backpack and runs downstairs to the kitchen where she sits in front of a huge, breakfast spread before her. Asil's father, Ken, walked in and takes his seat at the head of the table. "Good morning, daddy!" Ken smiled, 'Morning, pumpkin pie; come give your daddy a kiss!" Asil leaped out of her chair, hugging and kissing her father. Still cooking pancakes without turning around, Corynne interrupts, "Okay now, let's eat. You don't want to be late, and miss the school bus."

"No rush," says Ken, "Today is Asil's big day. Cheerleader tryouts! I'll take Asil to school today."

"Thank you, daddy." Asil says in-between bites. Asil's little brother, Devin, runs into the kitchen and sits down at the table. Corynne puts a good size plate of food in front of him. Corynne responds to Asil. "Oh, my goodness! I just don't want you to put yourself out there like that. You know how cruel kids can be!" Asil puts her glass of milk down. "Oh momma, please don't worry. Whatever they say, they going to say behind my back. I know how to take care of myself."

"I just don't want those mean girls making fun of you," Corynne replied as if she didn't hear what Asil had said. "Momma, they asked me to try out!"

Ken, while sounding a little protective, said, "Corynne, leave her be. Just because Asil is a little 'healthier' than the other girls…" Devin blurted out, "you mean fat," and started to laugh. Corynne glared at Devin, "Devin, could you do momma a favor?" "What momma?"

Corynne replies, "Eat your food and mind your business." Devin is still chuckling. Asil ignores Devin. Ken continues, "…that doesn't mean she is any less qualified." Asil to her mother, "Yeah, momma. Tasha said they need a strong base." Corynne puts her hand on her hip. "Why, because you're 'healthier' than the other girls?" Asil, looking at Devin, says, "You mean because I'm fat?" Devin smiled broad, but dared not say anything. Ken looked up from his plate, "We don't use that word around here." Devin's smile disappeared. "But they do use that word at school, daddy." Asil says, almost sounding defeated. Silence fell on the room. "Asil, eat. It's getting late." Corynne said as she breaks the silence.

CHAPTER TWO

Ken and Asil are finally in the car on their way to her school. Ken playfully poked Asil as she stares out of the car window. "So, pumpkin, have you been practicing for your tryouts?" Asil turned to a smiling Ken. "Oh, my goodness, dad. I have been practicing my jumps, splits and cartwheels. Daddy, guess what?" Ken looks intently at Asil, "What?" Asil shifts in her seat, "I can do a backflip!" Ken pumped his fist in the air, "See there! I knew you could do it. You are very athletic, just like me." Looking at her father with great interest, Asil asks Ken, Daddy, you played sports?" "Yup, I played football," Ken said with a certain amount of pride. Asil sits up in her seat. "Were you good?" she asked. Ken glanced at an eager Asil, "Sure was." he said, "but I had to work really hard at it. When I was your age, I was also very 'healthy.'" Asil looked intently at her dad, "Really? I thought you were always tall and skinny!" Ken began laughing. "Well, for that matter, your momma was a little thing when I first met her! Asil's eyes get real big. "I always thought I was healthy because of momma! Ken and Asil have a good laugh at that. Ken and Asil drive up to the front door of the school. Ken turns to Asil. "Pumpkin, you are too young to be worried about how much you weigh. I want you to have a fun childhood. I want you to have fun today. Asil looked at Ken, "I'm okay, daddy. Thank you for saying that, though." Asil opened the car door, gets out and looks back at her dad. "Don't worry about me, because I'm cute in the face and thick in the waist!" Ken looking surprised, "Where did you get that from? Asil just smiles at Ken. "Bye daddy!"

CHAPTER THREE

Asil has just changed out of her gym tights and back into her school outfit. Asil was able to squeeze in a short practice before

her first period. Asil was rummaging through her locker when her best friend Tara startled her from the other side of the locker door.

"Hey Central Middle School's newest cheerleader, my BFF Asil!" Tara brags.

"T, why are you so loud?" asked Asil, "Maybe you should be trying out for cheerleader!" "Who me? I am strictly a spectator." Tara proclaimed.

Twins and Central Middle School basketball stars, Kash and Ashton abruptly interrupt Asil and Tara.

"Hey, Tara. Hey, Asil." Kash greets the two young ladies. "What's up you two?" Tara put her hand on her hip to address the twins. "Excuse you, Kash! We were talking, thank you!

Ashton turned to Asil while trying to look in her locker. "Hey Asil, I know you got something in your locker to eat. Hook me up!

Tara and Asil look at each other with hands over their mouths. Asil slammed her locker shut. Ashton took a cautious step back while Asil stepped towards him. "What are you trying to say?"

Kash and Ashton look at each other and burst out laughing. Tara was the first to speak. "Excuse me, but what is so funny?"

Asil put her hand on Tara's shoulder. "I got this, T." Asil turned to Ashton. "Ashton, why are you looking for food in my locker? What, nobody cooks at your house?"

Tara and Kash laugh. Asil stops Kash mid-laugh. "Kash, I know you're not laughing over there with your ashy behind!"

Kash and Ashton walk off with Ashton yelling back at Asil, "Whatever Asil!" Kash looked back at Asil and said, "Good luck on your tryouts, Asil." Ashton adds, "Yeah Asil, good luck, cuz you're going to need it!" Kash shrugs, shaking his head at his brother, and runs off too.

Tara turned to Asil, "Don't pay those clowns any mind. I have to go to class 'Sil. Oh, and by the way, I think Kash likes you. See ya later." Asil, thought to herself,

"Kash likes me?" Asil is the only person left in the hallway.

CHAPTER FOUR

Asil is in the locker room about to put on her running tights for tryouts. Brandi and Tasha walked up to Asil. Asil braces herself for a verbal assault from the two cheerleaders.

Brandi is the first to speak. "Oh, my goodness Tasha, look who's really going to try out for the squad!" Tasha smirked at Asil, "Hey Asil. So, you ready to do this?" "As ready as you are." Asil snapped back.

Brandi, taking a cautious step forward, adds, "Well, I hope you haven't eaten anything in the past hour fatty. We don't want you getting sick on your stomach, or anything."

Asil took a somewhat aggressive step towards the two girls. "Oh, so now you're worried about my health? I got this. But thanks for your concern." Brandi and Tasha back up. "Well, excuse us for caring." The two cheerleaders turn and walked away then Asil changed into her tryout gear. Cheerleader coach Ms. Perks walked into the locker room. "Okay girls, let's hustle! Let's get out on the practice field."

Ms. Perks walked up to Asil. "Hey Asil, I'm so glad you decided to come out and show us what you got."

Asil, full of nervous energy, said, "I'm ready, Ms. Perks. Thanks for talking to me and supporting me." "That's what I'm here for, Asil." Ms. Perks moved in close as if to tell Asil a secret. "I was you when I was your age." "But you're so beautiful now," Asil responds.

Ms. Perks looked intently at Asil. "So are you, but you have got to believe that for yourself. Now get your rookie butt out there, and show off all the hard work you've put in." Ms. Perks turns and heads out the gym door and onto the practice field where the other cheerleaders began to gather. Asil takes a deep breath, looks around and heads out the gymnasium door.

CHAPTER FIVE

Just before Asil could step onto the field, she is met by Sheila and Leah, both who are also "healthy" girls. Sheila walks up and hugs a surprised Asil.

"Hey Asil, Leah, and I want to personally wish you the best on your tryouts." The more reserved and shy Leah speaks up. "That's right, Asil. I would never have the courage to do what you're doing." Asil hugged them both. "Thank you, guys. That really means a lot to me.

Ms. Perks blew her whistle that she wears around her neck. "Okay ladies, let's get lined up!" As Asil lined up with the other girls, she glanced into the mostly empty stands where she saw Tara, Kash, Ashton, Sheila and Leah sitting together ready to cheer her on. Tasha also saw them in the stands. She nudged Brandi and points toward the stands. "Awe, look, isn't that sweet? Asil's reject friends are cheering her on." Some of the girls snickered, but Asil pretended not to hear.

Ms. Perks addresses the girls. "It's good to see you all back. We have only one person actually trying out to hopefully round the squad out to ten. Asil, will you step forward and perform your prepared routine, please?" Asil can hear some of the girls chuckling. Some girls are smirking, and others are rolling their eyes. Asil looked at Ms. Perks. Ms. Perks nods her head for Asil to begin. Asil, full of energy, does her routine with great athleticism. She nails each movement with intense concentration, then ends her routine with an effortless backflip.

All of the girls, including Ms. Perks, watched in awe at Asil's performance. Asil's friends in the stands were yelling and cheering. Asil looked towards the gymnasium doors with joyful tears in her eyes.

To her surprise, her parents Corynne and Ken were there cheering and clapping for her. Ms. Perks blew her whistle and walked over to the deciding cheer committee and proclaimed, "All right, everyone. I think it is quite obvious that we are looking at our newest member of the squad, Asil!". All of the girls join in on the congratulations for Asil. Asil was smiling from ear to ear.

CHAPTER SIX

Asil, her brother Devin, and her parents are all sitting at the dinner table finishing up. Ken complimented his wife.

"Corynne, that was absolutely delicious!" Devin adds, "Sure was, momma!"

Corynne looks at everyone's plate. Asil had only eaten half her food. "Asil, why haven't you eaten all of your food?"

Asil quickly put her napkin over her remaining food. "Momma, it was just too much food. I have to watch what I eat. My uniform is already too tight." Ken took his plate to the sink. "Oh right, you got your uniforms today. Try it on and let's see how it looks." Corynne watched as Asil started up the stairs, eager to show her family her cheerleader uniform.

Corynne spoke up, Ken, it's starting already." Ken glanced over his shoulder at his wife. "No, you're starting." Corynne took a defensive stance. "What do you mean Ken?" Ken replied, "You know what I'm talking about." Corynne turned from Ken to the cluttered dinner table. "Not eating all her food and doing exercises before bed…It's just too much." Ken turned to his worried wife and gives her a hug. "Just let everything play out.

Asil is smart and she will find her balance." Before Corynne can respond, Asil comes running back down the stairs wearing her "too tight" cheerleader uniform.

Corynne is first to comment. "Oh no, that is simply not acceptable! Asil, you are only fourteen years old. That skirt is way too short.

Ken interjects. "What your mother is trying to say is that your outfit needs some fine-tuning."

"I don't need you speaking for me," Corynne said, It's bad enough I agreed to let her wear those ridiculous color lipsticks, and she's always cutting her shirts to have her shoulder out." Asil headed back up the stairs, "I know guys, but I have an idea of how to fix it."

Asil headed back to her room and sets up the sewing machine her grandmother bought for her birthday

Meanwhile, Ken and Corynne are wondering what Asil intends to do. The two finish cleaning up the kitchen. Ken sends Devin up to his room to get ready for bed, and Corynne is making a grocery list.

"Ken, maybe we should change the way we eat. Maybe we should just cut out meat altogether. I don't know. Am I a bad mother for cooking the way my momma did for us growing up down south?" Ken walked over to his wife and embraced her. "You are the most attentive, caring mother I know. I don't think we have to  drastically change the way we eat. If we just cut down on our portions and maybe cut out all these sodas, I think we might see a change over a period of time."

CHAPTER SEVEN

Just as Corynne is about to answer her husband, Asil comes trotting down the

stairs to show off her sewing talents. Asil is modeling and posing in a perfectly altered to shape cheerleader uniform.

Corynne took a walk around Asil, touching the hem while examining each stitch. "Asil, when did you get so good at sewing?" Corynne asked while motioning for Ken to examine Asil's uniform. "Wow, you must have really been watching your mother closely," Ken interjects.

Asil replied to her father. "Between watching momma and grandma, I've learned how to make my clothes work for me.

I already make improvements on everything you guys buy for me. I want to be a fashion designer that makes clothes to fit us 'healthy' girls one day." Corynne took a step back to kind of size up her daughter. "Asil, you sure that you don't mind showing off those big ol legs and arms of yours to the whole wide world?" she said sarcastically. Ken stumbled over himself to clean up his wife's blurted out statement. "Come on Corynne!" Ken says, trying not to sound too harsh. "You were doing so well!"

Corynne looked at Ken as if she had no idea of what he was talking about. "What did I say that was so bad?" Corynne asked, shrugging her shoulders. "I just commented on something of which she is quite aware, Ken,"

Asil responds before her dad can. "It's okay, momma. They talk about Serena too, and she's a champion!" Ken clapped his hands. "Bravo, Asil! Way to come back! Corynne heads towards the stairs then turns back to Asil and Ken. "I can't win with you two. You both just gang up on me. I'm tired now. I'm going to bed."

Corynne heads up the stairs in

a huff.

Ken sits at the table with Asil. "It's not fair but you are going to always have…and I hate to say this…haters. Even in your own family! Sometimes family can be the most critical without even meaning to be." Asil got out of her seat and went to her father. She gives him a big hug around his neck. "You know what, dad?" Ken looked his daughter in her eyes. "What, baby girl?" Asil took a deep breath. "Sometimes I get so tired of defending my size, altering my clothes and constantly having to make excuses for my thighs. Thank you for letting me rest from all that stuff." Asil gave her father a hug and goes up the stairs. Asil stopped halfway up the stairs and yells out to her dad, "Thick in the waist, cute in the face." Ken laughed and heads upstairs for the night. Asil goes in her room, buried her face in her pillow and cried herself to sleep in her uniform.

CHAPTER EIGHT

The next couple of months have been a dream for Asil. She is on cloud nine. Her life has changed so much since she decided to take control of her future and step out of her comfort zone.

Asil is now a respected member of the cheerleading squad, she is on top of her grades and getting better each day on her sewing machine.

Even some of the "mean girls" are being cordial. Best of all, her mom is not as uptight, and critical about her cheerleading because she has seen that Asil is one of the best girls on the squad.

Asil has changed her mindset after taking a leap of faith and believing in herself, not only did she feel good about herself, but other people couldn't help but show respect.

Asil also noticed she was getting a great deal of attention from Kash lately. Her

BFF Tara did mention to her that Kash liked her. Sometimes Asil would let her mind wander, and think about what it would be like if Kash truly did like her until a negative thought about her weight would sneak into her daydreams.

Anyway, Asil hasn't heard anything from Kash himself. Asil and Kash have known each other since they were in first grade, yet they have always just been friends. On this particular day, Asil was walking out of the school thanking the universe that things seemed as if they were officially turned around in her favor. Asil was feeling strong from all the new muscles being built from the cheer workouts and practices. She feels terrific, and couldn't ask for anything more. Just as Asil pushed through the double doors to exit the school, she felt a gentle hand on her shoulder. As she turns to see who it is, she finds herself face to face with Kash, and without his twin Ashton. Asil's mind was spinning because she was just thinking about him. As Asil looked up at Kash, he cleared his throat to speak, "Asil, I've been trying to catch up with you."

Asil's first impulse was to be her regular old guarded self, but she decided to answer him politely. "Oh really? So, you found me, what's up?" Kash cleared his dry throat again, "Well, I was wondering if you weren't already going with someone else, would you go with me to the spring dance?"

Asil was left frozen in complete shock. As she struggled to find the words to say yes, Ashton from down the hall yelled for his twin. "Hey, man, come on! We're going to be late for practice!"
Kash turned back to Asil, "Just let me know something when you decide." Before Asil can answer, Kash trots off toward Ashton then utters back to Asil. "I really hope you say yes." Asil was still stuck in cement as she watched Kash turn the corner. "Tara was right; he does like me."

CHAPTER NINE

Asil finally collected herself and snapped out of the trance. "Oh my God, what the heck am I supposed to wear?" Asil asked out loud.
Asil looked around to see if anyone spotted her having a conversation with herself. Asil immediately took out her phone, clicking on the calendar app. She gasped at the fact that she only has three weeks to figure out what in the world she was going to wear. Her mind was going in a million directions. "I could always wear black, but it's going to be too darn hot for black. I don't have anything in my closet, not even anything I could put into my sewing machine." So, Asil decides to go home and get the $60 that she saved from babysitting.
Then, she will go to the mall and find her perfect outfit for the spring dance. Asil decided to take her time upon arriving at the mall. "I'm not going to rush. I'm going to take my sweet time." She mumbled to

herself. Asil walked the mall for two hours. She saw a lot of things she liked. Some things she loved and some things her mother would like, but nothing which she would want to spend her hard-saved money. Finally, Asil stood in front of her mother and grandmothers favorite store: Fabrics, Prints & More. Asil took a deep breath and decided to enter the place that amazed and

sometimes overwhelmed her as a small child. Fabrics, Prints & More seemed like another world to Asil then.

She remembered back then feeling like being in a library when walking the many isles of fabric and spools of thread.

Women and girls were mulling over the colorful sea of fabric, cloth, and patterns. Asil had taken pictures of the outfits that she liked the most with her camera phone.

She compared different patterns to the pictures and studied the different textures of the spools of material lying in front of her. Asil headed to the cashier line to checkout. When her total added up to only $45, she knew that she had made the right decision. Asil was excited that she was able to select exactly what she wanted.

She could hear her grandmother say to her mother, "See, if you make your own clothes, you can only be mad at yourself if you don't like what you are wearing." Asil's mother would always say, "But momma, that's only something you would say to someone who can sew." They would always get a good chuckle out of that one Asil remembered.

As Asil was leaving Fabrics, Prints & More, she looked directly at Rayvulle Drug Mart

that's located directly across the aisle from where she was.

The store was advertising diet aids in their window. Asil walked across the way towards the store and stands in front of the window. Asil looked at the reflection of herself with the bottle of diet pills seeming to be her background in the reflection. "Look at my stomach. I lost a lot of baby fat, but I still got so much more to go. I've only got three weeks to get ready. I'm getting these pills. I don't care. I'm getting these diet pills." Asil walked into the drug store, finding the diet pills she saw in the window, and bought them.

CHAPTER TEN

Asil's parents and Devin had finished dinner by the time she arrived home from the mall. Asil's mother saw her first. "Hey Miss Asil, you're late for dinner. Where you been?" Asil lifted the bags from Fabrics, Prints & More.

Asil had already put the diet pills in her pocket.

"I decided to listen to you and grandma. I took a chance with the sewing machine." Asil said as she headed upstairs to her room. Asil waved at Ken and Devin. "Hey guys!" Asil said while on the move. Ken shouted out, "Hey, aren't you going to eat something?"

Asil replied, "No, I'm fine. I had a slice of pizza at the mall. Thanks anyway!" Asil put the bag with the fabric and patterns on her bed and then headed to the bathroom to get a glass of water.

Asil returned to her room and locked the door behind her with the glass of water and bottle of diet pills in her pocket.
Asil took out the bottle of diet pills, opened the child-proof top and shook two pills into the palm of her hand.

Asil looked up from the pills and into the mirror. As she undressed and stared at her reflection in the mirror, she thought about slimming down to just the right size after taking the diet pills. She fantasized about slimming down to maybe a size four while wearing a nice form-fitting dress with no rolls, nothing extra. But Asil started to think about the possibility of getting hooked on the pills and perhaps harming herself.

Asil tried to rationalize how she would only take one bottle and then be done with them for good. She just needed a jump start. Then, Asil thought about how disappointed her parents would be if they found out she was taking drugs. Asil stared at herself in the mirror.
She closed her eyes and opened her mouth, ready to take the pills. Suddenly, her father knocked on her bedroom door and startled Asil.

"Asil, is everything okay in there?" Ken asked through the door. Asil was frozen while staring at her reflection in the mirror with the pills in her hand.

STAY TUNED TO "THE LIFE OF ASIL" VOLUME 2 SOON!

THE LIFE OF ASIL Q & A

Do you think Asil will take the diet pills?
Do you think Asil will tell her father about the diet pills?
What do you think Asil will do, and why?

We would love to hear from you. Send us your thoughts, comments, and questions on The Life of Asil. Please feel free to contact us.
Email: TheLifeofAsil@gmail.com
Website: www.TheLifeofAsil.com
Instagram: @TheLifeofAsil
Facebook: @TheLifeofAsil
Twitter: @TheLifeofAsil

ABOUT THE AUTHOR

Asil Ttocs is a pseudonym of author Lisa Scott.
LISA is a true professional and is a incredible plus model who absolutely comes alive in front of the camera. LISA has had a lot of firsts in her long career as a plus model that opened the door and gave opportunity to many plus models who came behind her. She graced the pages of Essence Magazine editorial layout 4 times in the same year. She was the first and only plus size model to appear on BE Magazine where the response was so tremendous Belle Magazine was launched that catered to only plus size curvy women. She has appeared in Nordstroms, Belks, Avenue, Dress Barn, Dillard's, JC Penny, Macy's, Catherine's, Targets, to name a few and tons of catalogs. She was the first African American model to appear in Talk Magazine. She was the first African American model to appear on the cover Catherine's catalog and the first plus size African American model to book Seventeen Magazine. She has done several commercials and stood in for several years as Star Jones and Queen Latifah stand in on their commercials and movies. Her modeling travels have taken her as far as Mexico, Greece, St. Thomas and as close as the Hamptons. She has appeared on the View, Today Show, Fox Live and many more. She has worked every area of plus modeling print, fit, Informal and runway. She has walked the runway for Macy's, Lane Bryant, Full Figured Fashion week and BET Rip the Runway. She also has done many independent films and off Broadway plays.
Lisa resides in Dallas Texas with her family and blogs about plus size fashion, lifestyle and beauty as a hobby.
Instagram @theshoppingslayer

www.ingramcontent.com/pod-product-compliance
Lightning Source LLC
Chambersburg PA
CBHW041751040426
42446CB00001B/9